More Great Words of Our Time

**Thoughtful and
Provocative Comments
By Famous Men and Women
Of the 20th Century**

MORE
GREAT WORDS
OF OUR TIME

Edited by Tina Hacker

Hallmark Editions

Photo on page 28: Courtesy of NASA.

More Great Words of Our Time

Challenge is the core and
mainspring of all human activity.
If there's an ocean, we cross it;
if there's a disease, we cure it;
if there's a wrong, we right it;
if there's a record, we break it;
and finally,
if there's a mountain, we climb it.

JAMES RAMSEY ULLMAN

The purpose of life, after all,
is to live it, to taste experience
to the utmost, to reach out eagerly
and without fear for newer
and richer experience.

ELEANOR ROOSEVELT

In my belief, you cannot deal
with the most serious things in
the world unless you also understand
the most amusing.

WINSTON CHURCHILL

Young people searching for their
"real self" must learn that the real
self is not something one *finds*
as much as it is something
one *makes*; and it is one's daily
actions that shape the inner
personality far more permanently
than any amount of introspection
or intellection.

SIDNEY J. HARRIS

I think man has always gone
where he has been able to go,
and I think that when man stops
going where he can go he will have
lost a lot. Man has always been
an explorer. To me there's a
fascination in thrusting out and going
to new places. It's like going
through a door because you find
the door in front of you.

MICHAEL COLLINS

Do not look back. And do not
dream about the future, either....
Your duty, your reward —
your destiny — are *here* and *now*.

DAG HAMMARSKJÖLD

If only political leaders would
allow themselves to feel,
as well as to think, the world might
be a happier place.

GOLDA MEIR

As man develops the tools and
the capabilities to extend his reach
further and further, there is no doubt
we shall feel compelled to go as far
as we are capable of going.

EDWIN E. ALDRIN, JR.

The sea, once it casts its
spell, holds one in its net
of wonder forever.

JACQUES-IVES COUSTEAU

Knowledge is happiness,
because to have knowledge —
broad, deep knowledge —
is to know true ends from false,
and lofty things from low.

HELEN KELLER

When the body gets worn out,
the soul gets in shape.

POPE JOHN XXIII

We have to condemn publicly the
very *idea* that some people have
the right to repress others. In keeping
silent about evil, in burying it
so deep within us that no sign
of it appears on the surface, we are
implanting it, and it will rise up
a thousandfold in the future.

ALEKSANDR I. SOLZHENITSYN

Poverty is now
an inhuman anachronism.

HUBERT H. HUMPHREY

The young and the old are
closest to life. They love
every minute dearly.

CHIEF DAN GEORGE

I'm in favor of zero automobile
growth, otherwise known as ZAG.

RALPH NADER

To say "I love you"
one must know first
how to say the "I."

AYN RAND

Education is man's only hope.
Education is the imperative
of a universal and lasting peace....
Education is the key
that unlocks progress in the struggle
against hunger and want
and injustice wherever they may exist
on the earth. It is the path
which now beckons us toward
the planets and the stars.
Above all else, it is the wellspring
of freedom and peace.

LYNDON BAINES JOHNSON

I never eat in a restaurant
that's over a hundred feet off
the ground and won't stand still.

CALVIN TRILLIN

Where we have erred, let there be
no denial; where we have wronged
the public trust, let there be
no excuses. Self-criticism
is the secret weapon of democracy,
and candor and confession
are good for the political soul.

ADLAI E. STEVENSON

Religions are different roads
converging to the same point.
What does it matter that we take
different roads so long as we reach
the same goal? In reality
there are as many religions
as there are individuals.

MAHATMA GANDHI

I have a scheme for stopping war.
It's this — no nation is allowed
to enter a war till they have
paid for the last one.

WILL ROGERS

A good life is like a good play —
it has to have a satisfying
and exciting third act.

ETHEL BARRYMORE

Americans have always attached
particular value to the word
"neighbor." While the spirit of
neighborliness was important on the
frontier because neighbors were so few,
it is even more important now
because our neighbors are so many.

LADY BIRD JOHNSON

Less is more.

MIES VAN DER ROHE

God help the world on the day
when a Presidential council does not
have a man willing to face up
to the risks of peace.

HARRY GOLDEN

The history of free men
is never really written by chance
but by choice — their choice.

DWIGHT D. EISENHOWER

14

I don't think there's anything
better a man could say about
his life than that there's nothing else
he would rather be than what he is.

YOGI BERRA

We don't want wars even when we win.

GOLDA MEIR

A major distinction between
the athlete of today and those
of yesteryear is that the old
jocks rarely read books.
Today, some even write them.

HOWARD COSELL

In the tumult of men and events,
solitude was my temptation;
now it is my friend. What other
satisfaction can be sought
once you have confronted history?

CHARLES DE GAULLE

There is an exchange of thought
and feeling which is happy
alike in speech and in silence.
It is quietness pervaded with friendship.

HENRY VAN DYKE

The reason why worry kills more
people than work is that
more people worry than work.

ROBERT FROST

Unless we start to fight and
defeat the enemies in our own
country, poverty and racism, and
make our talk of equality and
opportunity ring true, we are
exposed in the eyes of the world
as hypocrites when we talk about
making people free.

SHIRLEY CHISHOLM

You must be like an oak tree —
your branches spreading out
widely so that the new saplings
may grow in their shade.
You must not be a beech tree,
growing so straight that you give
no shade to the next generation.

HAROLD MACMILLAN

Ideas are, of course, dangerous —
the most dangerous forces in the
world....The strength of democracy
lies in the freedom to express —
and to debate — ideas.

WILLIAM O. DOUGLAS

To give life a meaning
one must have a purpose
larger than one's self.

WILL DURANT

An excellent plumber is infinitely
more admirable than an
incompetent philosopher. The society
which scorns excellence in plumbing
because plumbing is a humble activity
and tolerates shoddiness in philosophy
because it is an exalted activity
will have neither good plumbing
nor good philosophy. Neither its pipes
nor its theories will hold water.

JOHN W. GARDNER

If two people who have been
strangers, as all of us are,
suddenly let the wall between them
break down, and feel close,
feel one, this moment of oneness
is one of the most exhilarating,
most exciting experiences in life.

ERICH FROMM

With knowledge and no faith,
we may well see a world destroyed.
With faith and no knowledge,
we may still see a world destroyed.
With faith and knowledge bound
together, we can hope to cherish
and protect the lives of the men
and the life of the world.

MARGARET MEAD

The last sound on the worthless
earth will be two human beings
trying to launch a homemade
space-ship and already quarreling
about where they are going next.

WILLIAM FAULKNER

Together, let us build sturdy
mansions of freedom, mansions
that all the world can admire
and copy, but that no tyrant
can ever enter.

JOHN F. KENNEDY

Courage is a special kind of
knowledge: the knowledge of how
to fear what ought to be feared
and how not to fear what
ought not to be feared.

DAVID BEN-GURION

Religion is believing in humanity
and trying to make it better.

INDIRA GANDHI

There is no human effort
that is not useful.
Everything counts.

SALVADOR DALI

God is really only another
artist. He invented the giraffe,
the elephant and the cat. He has
no real style. He just
keeps on trying other things.

PABLO PICASSO

23

Social progress and social justice,
in my judgment, are not something
apart from freedom; they are
the fulfillment of freedom.

ROBERT F. KENNEDY

Rumor travels faster, but it don't
stay put as long as truth.

WILL ROGERS

I'm proud to be called a politician,
for it's a great honor; when a
good politician dies he becomes
a statesman, and I want to be
a politician for a long time.

HARRY S. TRUMAN

Although I greatly prefer
nonviolence to violence, I prefer
freedom with violence to subjection
with nonviolence.

JAWAHARLAL NEHRU

24

I have found it impossible
to carry the heavy burden of
responsibility and to discharge
my duties as King, as I wish
to do, without the help and support
of the woman I love.

DUKE OF WINDSOR

Once a year, throw some money away.

WILLIAM SAROYAN

We start by being made by
others, and then we remake
ourselves, starting out from what
others have made of us.

JEAN-PAUL SARTRE

The upward course of a nation's
history is due in the long run
to the soundness of heart of its
average men and women.

ELIZABETH II

Always respect everyone's dignity
whatever his position. Especially
must we respect everyone's liberty,
for God himself renders that.

POPE JOHN XXIII

As life developed, I faced
each problem as it came along.
As my activities and work broadened
and reached out, I never
tried to shirk. I tried
never to evade an issue.
When I found I had something
to do — I just did it.

ELEANOR ROOSEVELT

Who knows about success?
You start with great faith,
know your limits and if you have
temperament and drive you will
eventually get somewhere. I didn't know
how far, but *somewhere*.

SOPHIA LOREN

All religions, arts and sciences
are branches of the same tree.
All these aspirations are directed
toward ennobling man's life,
lifting it from the sphere of mere
physical existence and leading
the individual toward freedom.

ALBERT EINSTEIN

Men will give themselves more
effectively if more
is expected of them.

FELIX FRANKFURTER

To sing is to love and to
affirm, to fly and soar, to coast
into the hearts of the people
who listen, to tell them that life
is to live, that love is there,
that nothing is a promise, but
that beauty exists, and must
be hunted for and found.

JOAN BAEZ

Perhaps going to the moon
and back in itself isn't all that
important. But it is a big enough
step to give people a new
dimension in their thinking —
a sort of enlightenment.

NEIL ARMSTRONG

Love one another,
but make not a bond of love:
Let it rather be a moving sea
between the shores of your souls.
Fill each other's cup
but drink not from one cup.
Give one another of your bread
but eat not from the same loaf.
Sing and dance together and be joyous,
but let each one of you be alone.

KAHLIL GIBRAN

I'm for any idea or movement
which looks to open any of us
to our potential bravery.

NORMAN MAILER

Great talents are the most lovely
and often the most dangerous fruits
on the tree of humanity. They hang
upon the most slender twigs
that are easily snapped off.

C.G. JUNG

Ultimate truth and ultimate
value will be reasonably attributed
to those ideas and possessions
which can give human nature, as
it is, the highest satisfaction.

GEORGE SANTAYANA

God must love housewives
as He does the poor.
He makes so many of us.

PHYLLIS MCGINLEY

The facts are that, notwithstanding
some failures in mechanism,
some blighted spots in the record,
our democratic institutions have
been working reasonably well, and
it is undeniably true that when real
trouble appeared to lie ahead, they
not only rose to meet the challenge,
but did so without sacrificing the
sacred tenets of our Constitution.

LEON JAWORSKI

What I feel like telling you
today is that the world needs
real dialogue, that falsehood
is just as much the opposite
of dialogue as is silence,
and that the only possible dialogue
is the kind between people
who remain what they are
and speak their minds.

ALBERT CAMUS

If the player on the other side
of the scrimmage line is as good
or better than you, you don't care
what color, religion or nationality
he is, you respect him.

JOHN WAYNE

Marriage is popular because
it combines the maximum of temptation
with the maximum of opportunity.

GEORGE BERNARD SHAW

Beyond peace, security and
prosperity lies a deeper universal
aspiration for dignity and
equal opportunity. Mankind will
never be spared all the tragedies
inherent in the cycle of life
and death. But we do have it
in our power to eliminate or
ease the burden of social tragedy
and of organized injustice.

HENRY KISSINGER

A thinking man feels compelled
to approach all life with the same
reverence he has for his own.
Thus, all life becomes part
of his own experience. From such
a point of view, "good" means
to maintain life, to further life,
to bring developing life
to its highest value.

ALBERT SCHWEITZER

God, apparently, did not want
a regimented world of sameness.
That is why creation is so manifold.

JOSHUA LOTH LIEBMAN

Throughout my adult life I have
believed in the perfectibility
of man. What a marvel he is —
what fantastic things he can do,
with himself and with the
world about him!

PABLO CASALS

Work has indeed been my best
beauty treatment. I believe in
hard work. It keeps the wrinkles
out of the mind and the spirit.
It helps to keep a woman young.
It certainly keeps a woman alive!

HELENA RUBINSTEIN

If one man offers you democracy
and another offers you a bag
of grain, at what stage of starvation
will you prefer the grain to the vote?

BERTRAND RUSSELL

Do we believe in the continued
growth of this country or do we
believe we have reached our
economic limit? All history and
every observation of your own eyes
proves that America is not finished.
It need never be finished.
There is no limit to America.

THOMAS E. DEWEY

I have nothing to offer
but blood, toil, tears and sweat.

WINSTON CHURCHILL

Industrialism produced a new
man — one adapted to the demands
of the machine. In contrast, today's
emerging consciousness seeks
a new knowledge of what it means
to be human, in order that the
machine, having been built, may now
be turned to human ends; in order
that man once more can become
a creative force, renewing and creating
his own life and thus giving
life back to his society.

CHARLES A. REICH

We are convinced that in our day
war is not inevitable. Man can
and must be relieved from
fear of its horrors.

NIKITA S. KHRUSHCHEV

The world has turned over many
times since I took the oath
on the plain at West Point, and
the hopes and dreams have
long since vanished, but I still
remember the refrain of one
of the most popular barracks ballads
of that day which proclaimed most
proudly that old soldiers never die;
they just fade away.

DOUGLAS MACARTHUR

A work of art has no
importance whatever to society.
It is only important
to the individual.

VLADIMIR NABOKOV

We are all, in the last analysis,
alone....We may delude ourselves,
but how much better to realize
that we are so.

ANNE MORROW LINDBERGH

We conclude that in the field
of public education the doctrine
of "separate but equal" has no place.
Separate educational facilities
are inherently unequal.

CHIEF JUSTICE EARL WARREN

I'm not afraid of growing old.
...It's a part one plays, and
we must all learn to play it.

RICHARD BURTON

A sad soul can kill you quicker,
far quicker, than a germ.

JOHN STEINBECK

I know of nothing more silly
than to expect "Government" to solve
our advanced problems for us.
If we have no ideas, how
can Government have any?

FRANK LLOYD WRIGHT

There are two things to aim at
in life; first, to get what
you want; and after that,
to enjoy it. Only the wisest
of mankind achieve the second.

LOGAN PEARSALL SMITH

I feel that the greatest reward
for doing is the opportunity
to do more.

DR. JONAS SALK

The world is in a miserable
state, and just on spite we ought
not to cry about it. And, if you
want to know the truth, that's
the source of my perpetually
good mood, my humor. Just
on spite, I'm not going to cry.
Just to spite them, there's
going to be laughter.

SHOLOM ALEICHEM

Woman must have room and
scope to devise a morality which
does not disqualify her from
excellence, and a psychology which
does not condemn her to the status
of a spiritual cripple.

GERMAINE GREER

Let me assert my firm belief
that the only thing we have
to fear is fear itself — nameless,
unreasoning, unjustified terror which
paralyzes needed efforts to convert
retreat into advance.

FRANKLIN D. ROOSEVELT

Black pride is a good idea —
but not as good as human pride.

WILT CHAMBERLAIN

Can you really love people,
care about people and give yourself
to them? Those are the things
that matter. And all the rest
is total delusion.

ERICA JONG

In war you do not have to be nice —
you only have to be right.

WINSTON CHURCHILL

One peak stands highest in
the ranges of human history.
One example shines forth of a people
uniting to produce abundance
and to share the good life fairly and
with freedom. One union
holds out the promise of justice
and opportunity for every citizen.
That union is the United States
of America.

GERALD R. FORD

Only within the moment of time
represented by the present century
has one species — man — acquired
significant power to alter
the nature of his world.

RACHEL CARSON

I feel...that each one of us
must have something in which he
believes with all his heart, so that
he need never be absolutely alone.

MARIAN ANDERSON

Education is a weapon,
whose effects depend on
who holds it in his hands
and at whom it is aimed.

JOSEPH STALIN

There is no record
that can't be beaten.

HOWARD HUGHES

Both the man of science and
the man of art live always
at the edge of mystery,
surrounded by it.

J. ROBERT OPPENHEIMER

Man should think of himself as a
ladder, placed upon the earth and
touching heaven with its head, and all
his gestures and affairs and speaking
leave traces in the higher world.

MARTIN BUBER